CHESS

CHESS

*An easy-to-follow illustrated guide to
playing this popular game of skill*

GARETH WILLIAMS

p

About the Author

Gareth Williams is an experienced chess player who has captained a number of London teams in England and he was a regular tournament and county player in the UK. He is an established chess teacher: for a number of years he has organized and coached children's classes at local schools. He is a regular contributor to the monthly magazine *Chess*, and is the author of *The Amazing Book of Chess* (1995). He is a founder member of Chess Collectors International and was elected its Vice President in 1984.

This is a Parragon Publishing Book
This edition published in 2000

Parragon Publishing
Queen Street House
4 Queen Street
Bath BA1 1HE, UK

Designed and produced by
Stonecastle Graphics Limited

ISBN 0-75254-256-7

Editor: Philip de Ste. Croix
Photographer: Andrew Dee
Hand model: Silvia Bucher

Note: the historical boards, pieces, and illustrations featured in this book are from the author's collection.

Manufactured in China

Contents

The Beginning

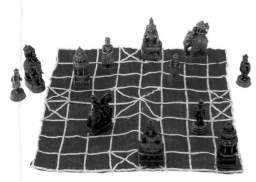

C HESS IS a game of war, believed to have been created more than 1500 years ago in India. It was then called *Chaturanga*, a name which referred to the four divisions of an Indian army consisting of war elephants, horsemen, war chariots, and foot soldiers. To these were added a Shah and a Farzin, the counselor to the Shah. Placed on an 8 x 8 squared board, two miniature armies carved from ivory faced each other ready to do bloodless battle on even terms, the skill of the opposing combatants deciding the result of the contest.

A print of an 18th century Indian painting showing two princesses playing chess.

An Indian cloth ashtapada *board. The carved ivory pieces (c.1790) come from Southern India.*

The game was an immediate success, stimulating the imaginations of the Shahs, their courtiers, and generals. It quickly spread to neighboring Iran where the game was introduced to the Arab invaders. The Arabs, in turn brought *shatranj*, the Arabic name for chess, to Baghdad where it was a favorite with the Caliphs, who by the 9th century employed their own court chess masters. In the 8th and 9th centuries, when the Moors invaded Spain, chess reached Europe. Chess was also brought to northern Europe by

An illustration from William Caxton's Game and Play of the Chesse *(1474) showing a philosopher using chess to teach wisdom and morality.*

Crusaders returning from their Holy Wars or Crusades, these knights having learned the game from their enemy, the Saracens. By the 12th century chess was firmly established as a favorite pastime throughout the feudal states of Europe.

At first there was little change in the Arabic rules of the game, even the Arabic names of the chessmen were

A Cambodian teak board, c.1820. The Islamic pieces are carved from ivory and horn.

maintained until the Renaissance. However, at the end of the 15th century, Spanish chess players began experimenting. The queen, who at the time could only move one square diagonally, was given the roving power she still has today, being able to move in any direction the full length of the board. The bishop's move was also enhanced, allowing it to move the length of the board along its diagonal. These changes resulted in a faster, more tactical and therefore more exciting game. The New Chess, or (as the Italians named it) Mad Queen Chess, spread rapidly throughout Europe. In the 500 years since then, there have only been a few additional minor modifications to the rules of chess.

A replica of a cushion board displaying late 18th century chessmen carved in Dieppe, France.

The Board

THE CHECKERED board is the battlefield for the two opposing chess armies. It has 64 squares set out as eight rows of eight. Similar boards were used centuries before the game of chess was invented, normally for simple chase-type games using counters and dice.

GETTING READY TO PLAY
In placing the board ready for the chessmen be sure that there is always a white square in the right hand corner, as illustrated. Remember – White on the Right.

Oleg Raikis created this board and box for the pieces in the 19th century Russian tradition.

In keeping with the martial tradition of the game, the squares going from left to right are called Ranks. Similarly the squares on the board stretching from bottom to top are known as Files. Naturally enough, the squares running diagonally across the board are called Diagonals. With the exception of the knight, all the chessmen move along either ranks, files, or diagonals.

THE CHESS SET
The popular chess set that nearly everyone plays with is known as a

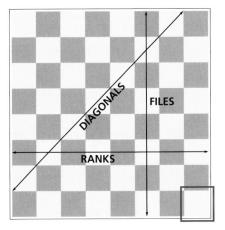

Chess sets are available in an infinite variety of forms, and decorative sets are often used as ornaments in the home. One of the best known of such artistic chess sets are the Lewis men. The original Lewis Chessmen were discovered on the Isle of Lewis, Scotland, in 1831. They represent a medieval Viking army dating from the 12th century. They can be seen at the British Museum in London. Other favored themes for chess sets are The Battle of Waterloo, Alexander the Great, Crusaders v Saracens, and Cowboys v Indians.

Staunton set. It is named after Howard Staunton, who between 1842 and 1851 was regarded as the best chess player in the world. The Staunton set was first sold commercially in 1849, and the design was immediately accepted because of the clarity of the individual pieces and their stability on the board.

The Staunton chessmen; this design was selected for international tournament play by the World Chess Federation in 1924.

The Lewis chessmen date from the 12th century. They are a fine example of a decorative set.

The Starting Position

B

TO SET out the chessmen to start a game, first place a white rook on the white square in the right-hand corner of the board and place the other white rook on the black square in the left-hand corner of the board. Then place on the first rank a white queen on the white central square (**A**). The king is then placed next to the queen on the black central square. The bishops are always placed next to royalty, so place one on each side of the king and queen (**B**). The knights are always placed on the square inside their castles/rooks (**C**). The pawns are placed on the next rank, one on each square (**D**). Repeat the same on the other side, starting on the eighth rank for the black side (**E**).

A

C

D

E

board, although, of course, pieces and squares may be made in many other colors.

Remember: rooks in the corners, with the first white rook on the white square in the bottom right-hand corner. This will also guarantee that the board is correctly placed.

Queens go on their own color in the central squares. Kings go next to queens in the center of the board.

Bishops stand next to royalty. Knights are positioned inside their rooks.

The expression Black and/or White is conventionally used in chess to identify and describe the opposing chess armies and the squares on the

The Rules of the Game

VALUE OF THE CHESSMEN

Before starting to play the game it is important to know the relative value of each piece. This will help you to understand whether it is advantageous to take an opponent's man or not. And also it will help you to decide when to exchange chessmen, i.e. whether to take advantage of those occasions when you can take a piece but thereby allow your opponent to capture one of your pieces in return.

A simple method is to use the pawns as the basic unit of "currency." If a pawn is regarded as one unit, the other chessmen can be valued as follows:

Queen ♕ = ♟♟♟♟♟♟♟♟♟

Rook ♖ = ♟♟♟♟♟

Bishop ♗ = ♟♟♟

Knight ♘ = ♟♟♟

However, when two of the main chessmen work together, their combined value is greater than the sum of the individual men:

Two rooks = ten pawns; they are stronger than a queen.
Two bishops = seven pawns; they are stronger than two knights.

These values should only be used as a guide, as, with experience, the relative position of the pieces on the board will be the prime factor to take into consideration before deciding the best move.

SOME BASIC RULES

Notice that the king is not given a value; as a fighting unit he is only stronger than a pawn, but as the main purpose of the game is to capture or **checkmate** the king, he is irreplaceable. Checkmate means the king has to be captured in such a way that there is no escape. If the king is threatened by an opposing piece, he must be warned by the attacking player calling "**Check!**" This allows the king the immediate option of escaping, defending himself, or capturing the threatening piece. If he cannot do any of these things, he is in checkmate and the game is lost. **This is the essence of chess.**

The first move in a game is always made by White. To choose which player has the white pieces, it is traditional for one of the contestants to hide a white and a black pawn in either hand. The other player points to one of the hands and whichever color pawn is revealed, that is the color he or she will play with for the first game. Subsequent games are played by alternating the colors between the two players.

Moves are taken in turn. You may not miss a move or make more than one move at a time. Once a piece has been touched, it must be moved. A move cannot be taken back and another one made instead. With the exception of checkmate, capturing is always done by the attacking chessman moving into the square of the captured piece and removing it from the board (**A**) (**B**). Capturing is optional: a chess piece under threat does not have to be taken.

The Moves of the Pieces

THE INDIVIDUAL pieces will now be dealt with in turn. The text provides a brief summary of their history and development, as well as explaining how each piece moves and captures opposing chessmen.

The Pawn

"Pawns are the soul of chess."
F-A.D. Philidor (1726-95), chessmaster and composer,
L'Analyze du Jeu des Echecs, 1748

19th century Austrian. *18th century English.* *18th century French.*

THE PAWN has always represented the infantry in chess, although in the Middle Ages Christian clerics attempted to "civilize" them by representing them as tradesmen, suggesting a different trade for each pawn. One might be a farm laborer, another a smith, others were merchants, gamblers, and even innkeepers. However, this image did not really catch on – the pawn as a foot soldier remains the favored model for most chess sets.

HOW THE PAWN MOVES

The pawns are individually the least powerful of the chessmen, but by working together they form the structure for defense and attack. The pawns move along their own files; on the first move the pawn has the option to move forward either one or two squares (**A**) (**B**), thereafter it moves forward one square at a time.

The pawn is the one piece on the board that cannot move backward. To capture the pawn changes direction and moves one square diagonally, in either direction (**C**). The pawn cannot take a piece on the square directly in front of it. In this case the pawn must remain static until the file is cleared, or it has the opportunity to capture by moving diagonally.

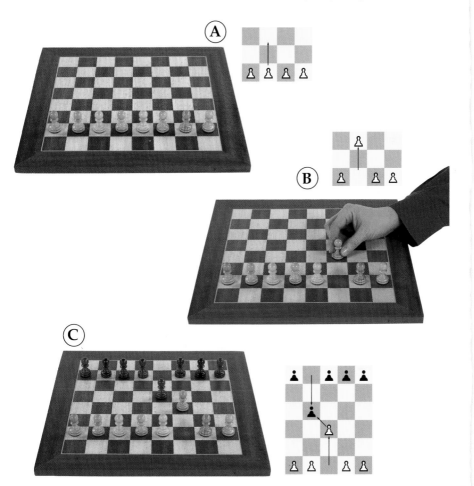

PROMOTION

When a pawn manages to fight its way right through the battle on the board and reaches the last rank (**A**), like any outstanding soldier it is promoted, and its player can choose to exchange it for any piece except the king. Of course, the normal choice is a queen (**B**), the strongest fighting piece on the board. Occasionally if the queen is still in play, then another piece can represent the extra queen. Usually this is a rook turned upside down. If no obvious chess piece is at hand, a coin or key will do to represent the extra queen.

EN PASSANT CAPTURE

This is an unusual pawn move that allows a black pawn on the fourth file to take an adjacent white pawn making its first move of two squares forward, as if it had only moved one square. And in reverse the white

Should the white pawn capture the black pawn?

8th rank

Answer: No. It should go for promotion.

 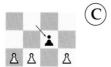 (C)

pawn can do the same to black. The attacking pawn actually passes diagonally behind the pawn it is capturing, which explains the term "en passant" – French for "in passing" (**C**). The easiest way to understand this is to study the photographs and diagrams above.

PRACTICE

Can the white pawn capture a piece?

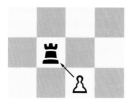

Answer: Yes, the rook.

UNDERSTANDING THE PAWNS

The formation of the pawns on the board is important to the outcome of the game. There are weak points to be avoided and strengths to cultivate. Here are some tips to remember when organizing your pawns.

• An isolated pawn: a pawn on a file that has no support from pawns on adjacent files can be easy prey for the opposing pieces.
• Doubled pawns: pawns of the same color on the same file can be difficult to defend and obstruct your attacking play.
• Passed pawn: a pawn with no opposing pawn on its file has better chances of promotion in the endgame.
• Pawn chain: pawns are strongest in a chain formation defending one another.

The Knight

"The knight, the cavalryman, the half forward, half sideways movement of the piece, resulting in strange combinations, make the knight the symbol and essence of chess."
Gustave Schenk, *The Passionate Game,* 1937

19th century Chinese. *19th century English.* *20th century Nigerian.*

HOW THE KNIGHT MOVES

The knight is the only chessman that can jump over another piece, whether friend or foe. To complicate matters slightly, the jump is done at an angle. This is the most troublesome of moves to learn but that is why it is also the most exciting. It makes the knight an excellent piece for springing an ambush.

THE KNIGHT originally represented the horse cavalry in the ancient Indian army. It has an unique jumping move that is exciting, often creating confusion among the chessmen on the board. Therefore, there has never been any temptation to consider altering the original move of this fighting piece. When the game first reached Europe, this piece had the Arabic name of "faras." In England it was renamed "knight," in France it is called a "cavalier," and in Germany a "springer," a name that is descriptive of the move it makes.

The knight does a two-step, but the first step is the jump, then, while up in the air, it moves diagonally in any direction. So if the knight is on a white square in a central position on

the board, it will cover eight black squares, and vice versa. Note that the knight does not capture the piece it jumps over, only the piece that is on the square it lands on (**A**)(**B**).

(A)

(B)

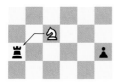

PRACTICE
Which piece can the knight take?

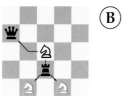

Answer: the rook.

Can the knight take the pawn?

Answer: No, but the pawn is threatening the knight which must jump away from it to safety.

THE KNIGHT'S TOUR
A good way to master the knight's move is to play a game of "solo." The purpose is to move the knight over the 64 squares of the board, visiting each square once. There are hundreds of different ways of solving this. And a knight may start the tour from any square. Here is one example:

50	11	24	63	14	37	26	35
23	62	51	12	25	34	15	38
10	49	64	21	40	13	36	27
61	22	09	52	33	28	39	16
48	07	60	01	20	41	54	29
59	04	45	08	53	32	17	42
06	47	02	57	44	19	30	55
03	58	05	46	31	56	43	18

The Bishop

*"Next stand two Mytred Bishops, who in war forget their calling,
vent'ring many a scar in Prince's cause, yet must no Bishops stray,
But leave the board, and keep the narrow way."*

John Wallis, *The Royall Game of Chess-Play*, 1693

19th century Chinese.	*18th century English.*	*"Medieval" theme: Italian.*

I N THE original Indian game the bishop was represented by a war elephant. In the Middle Ages, however, the elephant was barely known in England. The most authoritarian clique next to the monarchy were the bishops. As can be seen from the 12th century Lewis chessmen, bishops had established their place next to royalty, in the center of the English chessboard, at a very early date. In other countries the elephant was transformed into different figures: in France a fool, in

Italy a legionnaire, in Germany a messenger, and in Austria an officer.

The bishop, like the queen, benefited greatly when the rules were changed on the introduction of Mad Queen Chess (see pages 6-7). Previously the bishop was restricted to jumping over one square diagonally. The jump was eliminated and the bishop was allowed to move along the full length of the diagonal, in any direction, greatly increasing its influence on the game.

HOW THE BISHOP MOVES

The bishops move diagonally across

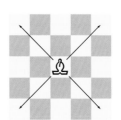

the corners of the squares. They can move in this manner as far as the edge of the board, unless their path is blocked by another chesspiece. Bishops cannot move along the ranks and files, neither can they jump over other chessmen.

When capturing, bishops move into the square of the captured piece, which is removed from the board (**A**) (**B**). Bishops always stay on the same color squares as the one they start on. They are referred to as "the white-squared bishop" and "the dark-squared bishop."

Can the bishop capture the black rook?

Answer: yes.

Can either bishop capture the other?

Answer: no, they are on different diagonals.

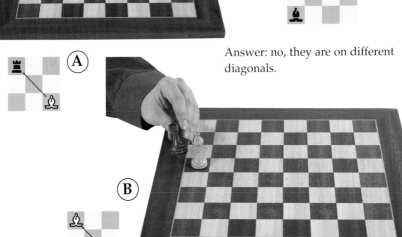

(**A**)

(**B**)

The Rook

*"Twenty-six families bear Chess Rooks in their coat of arms.
No other chess piece have been thus borne."*
Joseph Edmondson, *A Complete Body of Heraldry*, 1780

19th century German.   *16th century Egyptian.*   *14th century Russian (copy).*

RUKH IS an old Indian word meaning chariot. Historically chariots as used in battles went out of fashion in the 5th century, and the fact that rooks/chariots were used as part of the game of chess has led to speculation that chess may have been played in this era or possibly even earlier! In 1527, a Bishop of Alba wrote a famous poem about chess. In the poem he described the rooks as "warring towers bourne on the backs of elephants." This description was taken up by the carvers of decorative chess sets who represented them as

an "elephant and castle." In playing sets the design was reduced to the more practical size of a castle or tower.

The rooks have since the beginning maintained the same move and until the queen obtained its increased powers in the 16th century, the rooks were the most effective chessmen on the board.

HOW THE ROOK MOVES

The rook moves in straight lines along the ranks and files. The rook can choose to move over as many squares as are empty, to its front,

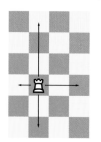

back, left, or right, in one move. Rooks can never move in a diagonal fashion, neither can they jump over other chessmen. When capturing, the rook moves into the square of the captured piece, which is removed from the board (**A**)(**B**).

Is it safe for the rook to capture the knight?

PRACTICE

Which piece can the rook take?

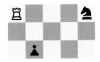

Answer: the knight.

Answer: no, the bishop protects the knight.

23

The Queen

"That thou mayst be a Queen, and check the world."
William Shakespeare, *King John* (1623)

19th century
English.

18th century
Danish.

19th century
French.

O VER THE years the queen has switched gender! Originally (s)he played her part on the board as a Farzin, a wise man who counseled the king. His powers were restricted to moving only one square in a diagonal direction. When chess came to Europe this chess piece was known as a "fers," a corruption of the Persian "farzin." In medieval European culture it was accepted that the person next to a king should be a queen. Two sets of chessmen have survived from that time, the Lewis chessmen in the British Museum and a group of figural chessmen kept at the Bibliotheque Nationale in Paris; both show queens seated on a throne. Thus, the change of gender from male to female had come about, although the name "fers" continued in currency for a few hundred years more.

However, the lady had to wait until the Renaissance to obtain the chessboard power that she enjoys today. Changes to the rules occurred when experiments were tried in Spain to speed up the game. One such change increased the power of the queen so that she could move in any direction the length of the board. This resulted in Her Majesty becoming the real power behind the throne and the game being re-christened by the Italians the "Mad Queen Game."

HOW THE QUEEN MOVES
The queen is the most forceful chesspiece on the board. It moves the length of the board in any direction

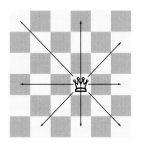

along the diagonals, the ranks, and the files. Because of this fearful power, it is important that you do not carelessly allow the piece to be taken. Losing your queen usually means losing the game. The queen captures by moving into the square of the captured piece, which in turn is taken off the board (**A**)(**B**).

In this example (**C**) a queen can capture a rook on the diagonal, or a bishop along the file, or a knight along the rank.

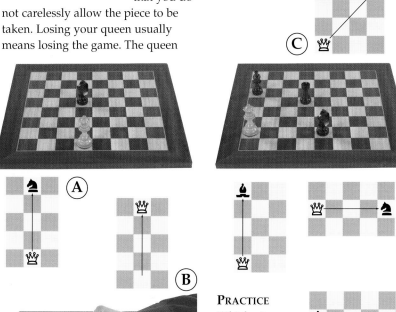

A

B

C

PRACTICE
Which piece does the queen capture?

Answer: the knight.

The King

19th century Indian.　*18th century French.*　*19th century Austrian.*

HOW THE KING MOVES

The king is the most important piece on the board. The king cannot be taken as other pieces can – when threatened, a warning must be given by saying "Check." The aim of the game is to trap the king in such a way that he cannot escape; then he is "Checkmate." The word comes from the old Persian phrase "Shah-mat," meaning the king is dead. How the king can be checkmated will be explained on pages 30-33.

ORIGINALLY, IN India in around 600 AD, the king was revered as a Shahanshah, an Emperor or King of Kings, worthy of respect, protection, and even worship. This is the king on the chess battlefield, weak as a simple pawn because only able to move one square at a time, but demanding the respect of a god. For if the King is captured or killed, the Empire (or game) is lost.

Kings can only move one square at a time, but in any direction. To capture an opposing piece the king moves into its square and the piece is taken off the board (**A**)(**B**). When the king is in check (**C**), it

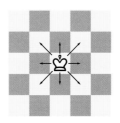

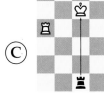

must respond. This can be done in a number of ways:

• The piece giving check can be taken (below).

• The king can move out of check on to an adjacent square (left).

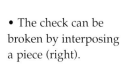

A king can never move into a square where he would be in check. Because of this, opposing kings can never be on squares adjacent to one another.

• The check can be broken by interposing a piece (right).

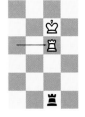

Castling

THIS IS a special move introduced in the 16th century permitting the king and rook both to make a move at the same time. The purpose was to speed up the game, safeguard the king and develop the position of the rook all in one go. This move can be made on either side of the board: moving to the right is known as castling "king-side," moving to left is castling "queen-side." The king has to be moved first, and the actual maneuver results in the rook being moved to the adjacent square to the king in the center of the board and His Majesty being placed on the other side of the rook. To castle king-side (**A**) the king is moved two squares to the right (**B**) and the rook is moved to the other side of the king (**C**). To

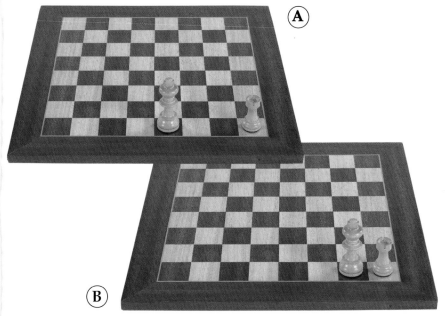

(C)

castle queen-side, the king is moved two squares to the left and the queen-side rook is moved round to its other side (**D**).

There are certain rules regarding castling that have to be understood:

• Castling cannot be done if the king

or rook have previously been moved during the game.
• The king cannot castle out of check.
• The King cannot castle into check.
• The King cannot castle by passing through check.
• To castle the squares between the king and rook must be unoccupied.

(D)

29

Checkmate

IN ORDER to win a game of chess the king has to be **checkmated.** This can be done as quickly as in two moves, known as "Fool's Mate," but normally it is achieved after a battle lasting 25 moves or more, when only a few men are left on the board to fight out the "endgame." Remember the king may not be captured – when the king is threatened by an opposing piece, a warning must be given by saying "Check." The king must respond to this immediately by getting out of check. If the king discovers that he is unable to protect himself, either by moving out of check, or interposing one of his own men, or by capturing the threatening piece, then the king is checkmated. The king is dead, and the battle lost, no matter that the losing side may have more chessmen left on the board or seemingly be in a better position.

OBTAINING CHECKMATE

It is "checkmate" that has made chess the exciting and interesting game that it is. Other board games do not have this dimension that allows for stimulating tactical combinations, including imaginative sacrifices of a part of one's army in order to trap the opposing king in checkmate.

In order to obtain checkmate certain conditions have to be accomplished:

• The king has to be in check.
• The king cannot move to an adjoining square.
• The king has no man that can be interposed to break the check.
• The king has no man that can capture the checking piece.

When this is achieved it is checkmate, and the game is over. Reset the chessmen for the next game.

FORCING CHECKMATE

The strongest pieces in chess are the queen and the rooks. They are referred to as **major pieces.** They are the only individual pieces that, with the help of their king, can force checkmate on a cleared board. It is important to remember that when in the endgame there are only a few pieces left on the board, in order to win you will need a queen, a rook, or

a pawn that can be promoted, so that a "mate" can be achieved.

CHECKMATE WITH KING AND QUEEN

A king and queen working together can force the opposing king to the side of a board and force mate.

The black king having been forced to the edge of the board (**A**) is mated

by the white queen which is protected by the white king (**B**).

CHECKMATE WITH KING AND ROOK

A king and rook have to work patiently to force an opposing king into a corner of a board where it can be mated (**C**).

The white king and rook force the black king into a corner until the rook is able to mate the black king trapped between the white king and the edge the board.

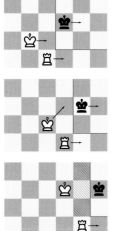

On the previous page it was explained that the queen and rook are vital in the endgame because they are the only individual pieces that can force mate with the help of the king. This is where the ability to promote a pawn becomes so crucial: if you can turn a simple pawn into a queen, the game can be won.

PROMOTING A PAWN
If only a pawn and the kings remain on the board it may be a simple matter of the pawn racing the opposing king to the eighth rank. This can be measured by visualizing a "square" on the board from the pawn's position to calculate which piece will arrive first at the vital square on the eighth rank. If the king is outside the imaginary square with the pawn to move, then the pawn will win the promotion race.

But if not, then the king must be used to support the pawn's progress. The white king protects the vital squares to allow its pawn to move through to the eighth rank.

CHECKMATE WITH OTHER CHESS PIECES
Checkmate can happen at any stage of the game, here are some recurring examples of one move mates.

Smothered Mate
In one move the knight has taken a pawn and mated the king trapped by its own men (**A**)(**B**).

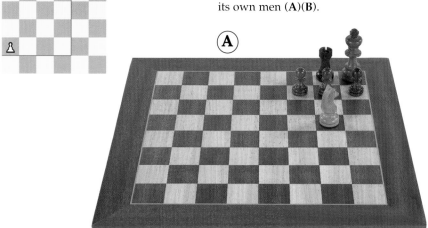

B

Pawn Mates King
One square forward and the humble pawn wins the game.

Bishop Mates King
Bishop mates with covering help from the rook to outsmart the black queen (**C**)(**D**).

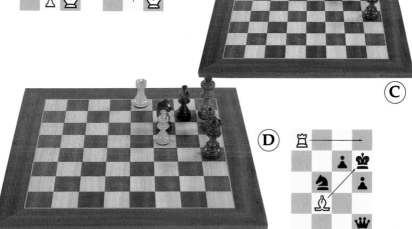

C

D

Drawn Games

OF COURSE not all chess games are won or lost. Games played between chess masters are often drawn due to their playing strengths being approximately equal. There are a number of ways the game can be drawn.

• Insufficient chessmen.
If only the kings are left on the board, this is an obvious draw. But neither can a knight and king win against a king, nor a bishop and king against a king.
• Perpetual check
If a position is reached where the king can be repeatedly checked, it need only occur three times for the game to be a draw.
• Repetition of position
This is a very rare occurrence when the same position on the board happens for the third time; it does not have to happen consecutively for the draw to apply.
• Fifty move rule.
A draw can be claimed when no pawn has been moved and no capture made for over 50 consecutive moves.
• Stalemate
This comes about when the king is not in check, but any move by him will place him in check. This is a draw by stalemate.

In each example (**A**)(**B**)(**C**) the black king is to move but he cannot go anywhere without moving into check, which is not permitted in chess. Stalemate! Drawn game.
• Agreed Draw
In tournament chess players can by mutual consent agree a drawn game. With their experience they can assess that the game has reached a certain stage at which the most probable result will be a draw.

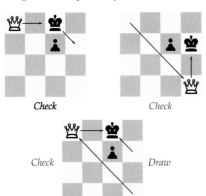

Check

Check

Check

Draw

Chess Notation

THE GAME of chess has its own literature and records. For over a thousand years some of the outstanding chess problems, games, and studies, the legacy of great chess masters of the past, have been recorded and preserved through a system of notation developed to register chess moves. The first practitioners were Arabic chess players of the 9th and 10th centuries who created their own Algebraic method. Then, when chess came to Europe, a different method developed called the "Descriptive System." In the 18th century a Syrian chess master, Philip Stamma,

introduced another algebraic system which he used in his 1745 book *The Noble Game of Chess*. Since then both systems were used until 1976 when the World Chess Federation (chess's governing body) decided to recognize only one system of notation for chess tournaments and matches. They decided on the Algebraic system which is now referred to as "Standard International Chess Notation."

STANDARD NOTATION

Once this system of notation is understood, games and problems can be studied in books on chess, and games printed in newspapers and magazines, often those played by International Grandmasters, can be followed and analyzed. A knowledge of this notation will help to improve your standard of play, enabling you to examine and appreciate chess masterpieces and the genius of gifted players.

Each square is identified by two co-ordinates (left). The letters a to h are shown left to right, one letter for each square, on the lower horizontal edge of the board to identify each file.

	a	b	c	d	e	f	g	h	
8	a8	b8	c8	d8	e8	f8	g8	h8	8
7	a7	b7	c7	d7	e7	f7	g7	h7	7
6	a6	b6	c6	d6	e6	f6	g6	h6	6
5	a5	b5	c5	d5	e5	f5	g5	h5	5
4	a4	b4	c4	d4	e4	f4	g4	h4	4
3	a3	b3	c3	d3	e3	f3	g3	h3	3
2	a2	b2	c2	d2	e2	f2	g2	h2	2
1	a1	b1	c1	d1	e1	f1	g1	h1	1
	a	b	c	d	e	f	g	h	

The numbers 1 to 8 are similarly shown on the left-hand vertical edge of the board, identifying each rank. These markings are often printed on boards as an aid to recording a game. Diagrams of boards will always show White playing from the first rank and Black from the top (8th) rank.

The chess pieces are identified by the initial letter of each piece, with the exception of the knight which, having the same initial letter as the king, is shown as N.

In practice, the P for pawn is not normally used, the board co-ordinates being sufficient to identify the piece, i.e. e4 means that a pawn moves to occupy the square e4.

Certain other symbols are used to signify other events in the game:

x Capture
+ Check
++ Checkmate
= Pawn promotion
o-o King-side castling
o-o-o Queen-side castling
? Bad move
! Good move
... Black to move
e.p. en passant

When using standard notation to record a game, the moves are numbered from 1 onward. If the move is a pawn move, only the co-ordinates of the square to which it moves need be stated – e4 means a pawn has moved on the e file to the 4th square on that rank. If, for instance, a bishop had made the move, the initial letter of the piece is used to identify it and it is written as Be4. If the bishop was capturing on that square it would be recorded as Bxe4. There is no need to mention which piece has been captured. When two similar pieces, such as two knights, can move to the same square, then the departure square is recorded to clarify which piece is meant: Nbd7 means that the knight on the b file has moved to square d7.

To provide a simple example of using notation here is the shortest game it is possible to play, Fool's Mate.

white	black.
1. g4	e5
2. f3	Qh4++ (checkmate)

Early chess notation: an illustration from an 18th century Italian instructional manuscript.

Tactics

Tactics ARE the heart of the middle game. By knowing the simple tactical maneuvers that the chess men are capable of, and by creating combinations from their basic moves, you will soon discover that chess has a special quality missing from most other board games.

There are some general themes that occur repeatedly in play, and with practice they will become familiar and easy to recognize, allowing you to plan some satisfying tactical traps for your opponent to fall into. The most frequently used tactics are the fork, the pin, and the skewer. These are often combined in lines of play known as the discovered attack, overloading, and the sacrifice. Each will be examined in the following pages and the examples illustrated will explain and show how effective these ploys are. Remember: most chess games are won through tactics.

THE FORK
This is a tactic that each piece can employ whereby two or more opposing chessmen are attacked simultaneously. This double-pronged assault means that one of them has to be lost. In the first example we see how a lowly pawn can fork more valuable pieces.

Pawn Forks Rook And Knight
The way a pawn captures diagonally allows it to fork simultaneously in two directions. Here a rook and knight are both threatened; one has to be taken (**A**)(**B**).

(**A**)

Knight Forks Rook And Queen

The fork is the only tactic a knight can employ. From a central square it can fork onto eight different squares. As this is combined with its characteristic angled jump, the result is that the knight fork is well disguised, making it a very dangerous attacking piece for the middle game (**C**)(**D**).

(**B**)

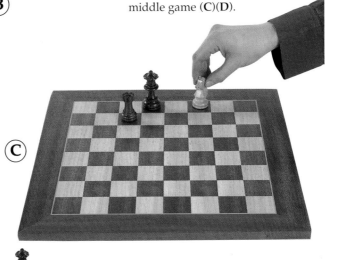

(**C**)

(**D**)

Powerful pieces like the queen, the rook, and the bishop can move freely across the board in several directions. This makes them particularly useful when it comes to setting up attacking forks. Even the king can develop a fork, as we see on these pages.

Bishop Forks Two Rooks

The bishop is always on the lookout for forking opportunities on the diagonals. Here two rooks suddenly find themselves under threat. One will be taken (**A**)(**B**).

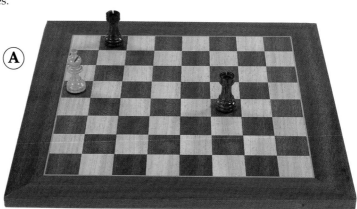

(**A**)

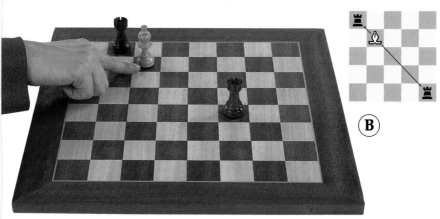

Rook Forks Bishop And Knight

Working on both files and ranks the rook can often trap two pieces in a fork (**C**)(**D**).

(**C**)

(**D**)

Queen Forks Bishop, Knight, And Rook

The fork shows how powerful the queen is because of her ability to rove along ranks, files, and diagonals. Here three pieces are caught in a fork.

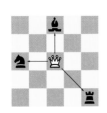

King Forks Rook And Knight

Even the king can effectively fork the opposing pieces.

The Pin and the Skewer

THE PIN is a direct attack on one piece and an indirect one on another, both being on the same rank, file, or diagonal. The first chessman is pinned because if it moves, the second (more valuable) piece will be exposed to capture. The pieces that can achieve this are the queen, rook, and bishop. The illustrations show examples of pins.

Here the queen pins the black bishop against the king (**A**). The bishop cannot move as the king would then be in check. So it can be captured by the white queen on the next move.

In this example (**B**), the rook has pinned the black knight against a bishop; one of them will be taken on the next move.

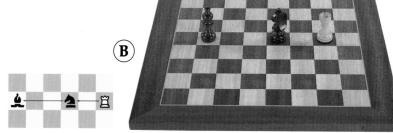

A

B

The bishop can pin along the diagonals – here a knight is pinned against a rook (**C**). The knight can be taken with the next move.

THE SKEWER

The skewer, like the pin, is an attack on two pieces on the same line. One piece is "skewered" behind another more valuable piece.

In the example illustrated a protected rook skewers the black queen against the king (**D**). Although the queen is able to take the attacking rook, she will be lost to the white bishop on the next move, and the capture of a rook is not sufficient compensation for the loss of a queen.

Discovered Attack and Overloading

THE DISCOVERED attack is an ambush, or double attack, which is particularly effective if a "check" can also be given at the same time. It occurs when a piece is moved to allow another piece on the same side to attack an opposing piece.

In this example (**A**) the white bishop moves to attack a knight while at the same time allowing the rook stationed behind to check the black king (**B**). The king must move out of check and the bishop can then capitalize on the situation by capturing the knight.

Here (**C**) the knight moves giving a discovered check on the king by the bishop, and at the same time threatens a rook, which will be captured on the next move (**D**).

A

B

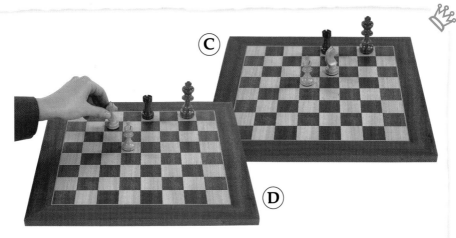

© D

E

OVERLOADING

A defending piece may find itself protecting more than one of its own chessmen. An attack on these pieces can cause the defending side to be "overloaded." If one piece is captured, the recapturing of the attacker will leave the other piece undefended.

In this example (**E**) a black knight is defending a bishop and a rook; both are under attack, the rook by the white queen and the bishop by a rook. Normally a rook would not be sacrificed for a bishop, but in this case when the knight has captured the rook, the black rook is no longer protected and is taken by the queen.

The black queen in the diagrams (right) is overloaded protecting two pieces which are under attack; a piece must be lost.

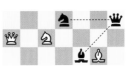

1. BxN

2. ...QxB
3. NxB
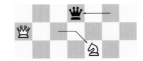

Sacrifice

THIS IS the ultimate tactic in chess. You apparently give a piece away, but it is in order to obtain a greater advantage some moves farther on in the game. You may gamble to win or lose on one move, to deliver a knockout punch in the height of battle, and even make the supreme sacrifice of all, a queen sacrifice, on the expectation of ultimately gaining checkmate.

Here is an example of a queen sacrifice (**A**)(**B**)(**C**).

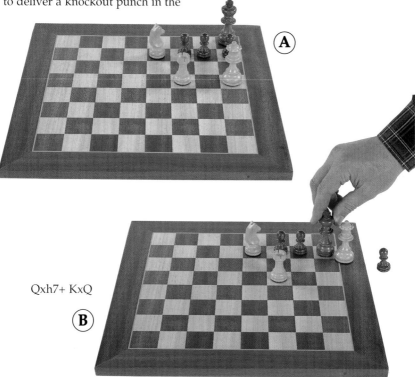

A

Qxh7+ KxQ

B

Rh5++

In this second example (right) a bishop sacrifice is made to break up the black defense in front of the king and allow the white queen and rook to checkmate in two moves (below).

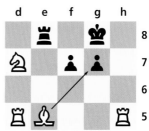

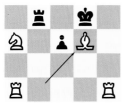

Bxg7

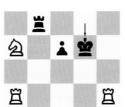

...KxB

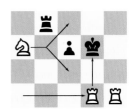

Rdg5 ++

Tactical Tips

RUY LOPEZ, a 16th century Spanish priest and the best chess player of his day, recommended that the board should be placed so that the sun would shine in the eyes of an opponent! Still good advice, but these days most chess is played under electric lights and the players have to rely more on their own powers of concentration than on grabbing the better seat.

Initially it is important to play as frequently as you can to become familiar with the moves and the rules. Avoid being careless by leaving a piece *en prise*, i.e. in a position where it can be taken with no compensating advantage accruing to you. Study this book for reference, and as problems arise check the book. Use it for practice. When studying a game use two chess sets, one to

toward the end of the game when their longer range on the diagonals gives them the greater effectiveness.

• Rooks are also most useful when the board has been cleared of most of the pieces, and they can work along the open files and ranks.

• Pawns are strongest in protective chains but isolated pawns make easy targets.

• The king can be used in an attacking mode in the endgame.

• The best way to improve is to play frequently and to study simple checkmates and tactical positions. This will rapidly provide you with a good understanding of the varying strengths of the pieces and help you to develop an ability to calculate some moves ahead.

• The more you study, the more you win games, the more fun it is to play more games. And one day you too could be a Grandmaster.

follow the main line of play and one on which you can analyze the position to understand the ideas of the players and try out different ideas or lines of play.

Try to develop the habit of concentration. Before each move, think! Look at the position of the pieces on the board – is there a move that can improve your game, or is your opponent threatening material that needs to be defended! The more time taken to assess the position, the more information is absorbed through your eyes and passed to your mind, which helps you decide on a commonsense reply.

TOP TIPS

• Knights come into their own in the middle game when they can jump into complicated positions.

• Two bishops are better than knights

Starting a Game

WHEN STARTING a game it is important to move the chess men into good positions ready for the main battle. Understand the basic plan of obtaining control of the center of the board, either by placing pawns on the central squares or by having pieces aiming their power toward the center threatening the opposing pawns or pieces occupying those squares. To help you understand opening strategy, follow the notation of this example game. My comments describe the aim of the moves.

This game was played between two English Grandmasters at an important tournament held in Tilburg, Netherlands, November 1998.
White: Matthew Sadler.
Black: Michael Adams.

Nimzo-Indian Defense. (A number of popular openings that are used frequently are given names to identify the sequence of moves used. Nimzo-Indian is one such.)

1. d4 Nf6
White has placed a pawn on a central square and opened the diagonal for the bishop to use. Black develops a knight and discourages white from playing e4 on the next move to start occupying the central squares.

2. c4 e6
White has placed another pawn centrally and Black replies defensively with a pawn move but opens attacking lines for the bishop and the queen (**A**).

(**A**)

(B)

4. e3 b6

White moves another pawn to strengthen the center. Black also moves a pawn ready to develop the queen-side pieces to attack the center (**B**).

5. Bd3 Bb7

Both bishops are moved to squares where they aim at the center, but the black bishop is also threatening to take the g pawn.

6. Nf3 0-0

White develops the other knight and protects the threatened pawn. Black castles, moving the king to a safer location and bringing the rook into the center (**C**).

3. Nc3 Bb4

A knight is developed to cover the central squares and Black replies by developing his bishop, pinning the knight against the king.

(C)

7. 0-0 Bxc3
White castles and Black exchanges a bishop for a knight defending the center.

8. bxc3 c5
White recaptures the bishop. Black attacks for control of the center with a pawn thrust (**A**).

9. a4 d6
White moves the a pawn to gain space on the queen's wing. Black

gains equality of position with a pawn placed toward the center.

10. Ba3 Ne4
White completes its development by moving a bishop off the first rank and thereby connecting rook and queen. Black attacks in the center occupying a square and threatening the backward doubled c pawn (**B**).

(A)

(B)

Only two pieces had been taken while both players fought for control of the center while simultaneously developing their pieces onto active squares creating fighting opportunities for their game. At this stage the position is judged as being equal for both players. The game was eventually won by Matthew Sadler on the fortieth move when Michael Adams resigned as his queen was about to be taken.

When starting a game remember what these grandmasters were determined to achieve in the example we have just studied:

• Development of pieces quickly onto squares where they can be most active.
• Continued development until each piece is in play and the king has castled.
• Control of the center, either by placing pawns there or by pieces aiming there.

A Master Game

THE NEXT section introduces you to a complete game played in 1997 by two expert players, both International Masters. By following the chess notation and the accompanying illustrations you can learn a lot. Each move is explained to help you gain an understanding of the position and the plan that each player had in mind. Playing with the white pieces was 14-year-old Luke McShane. His opponent, Graham Lee, was an experienced tournament player and a chess coach to many young talented players, such as his opponent in this game.

The opening is called the French Defense. It became popular after 1834 when it was used by a winning Paris team in a correspondence match against London.

1. e4 e6
White places a pawn in the center. Black's e6 is the move that gives this defense its name. Note that the diagonals for both sides have been opened so that the queens and bishops can move across the board.

2. d4 d5
Both sides contest the center ground.

3. Nd2 dxe4
White develops a knight. Black captures a central pawn (**A**).

(**A**)

4. Nxe4 Nd7
The pawn is taken by the knight while Black develops one of his knights.

5. Nf3 Nf6
Development of the knights toward the center continues.

6. Nxf6+ NxN

An exchange of knights maintains the equality in the center (**B**).

7. Bd3 b6

White brings a bishop out where it can cover the empty e4 square. Black's reply is to make room for the bishop on b7 where it will also be covering the e4 square.

8. 0-0 Bb7

White moves his king away from the center while bringing the rook into play. Black continues his plan of development and pressure on the center.

9. b3 Be7

Both players continue to develop their positions (**C**).

10. c4 0-0

The opening phase is nearly over with both sides having castled and moved their pieces onto squares where they have greater potential than they had in the starting position.

11. Bb2 c5

The battle is still about control of the center, but note that White also has pressure building up on the king side. The knight is placed there and the bishops, although positioned on the queen side, are aiming through the center toward the pawns in front of the black king.

12. dxc5 bxc5

White exchanges pawns to create an open center in preparation for an attack on the black king's defenses (**A**).

13. Qe2 Qc7

The queens are moved to better squares, and their rooks are connected.

14. Rad1 Qc6

A rook is centralized. The black queen plans to meet White's attack with a counterattack. Note that if the white knight were to move to e5, Black would checkmate with Qxg2.

15. Qe5 Rfd8

Both sides are still maneuvering to improve their attacking chances (**B**).

(**B**)

(**A**)

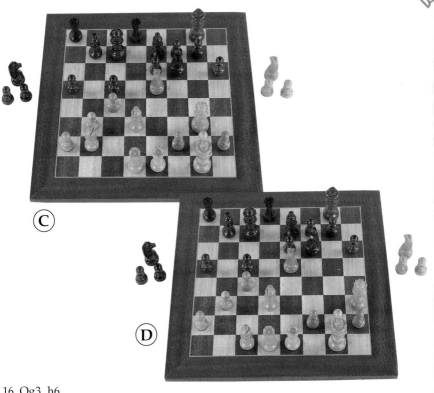

(C)

(D)

16. Qg3 h6
The tension grows; there are combinations being threatened.

17. Rfe1 a5
White brings the rook onto a central half-open file. Black plays a waiting move.

18. Ne5 Qc7
White is now forcing Black onto the defensive (**C**).

19. Bc1 Nh5
White decides his bishop can attack better from c1. Black tries to chase the white queen away.

20. Qh3 Nf6?
The queen moves out of the threat from the knight. The knight moves back to a defensive position, overlooking White's sacrificial reply (**D**).

21. Bxh6! gxh6

White gives the bishop away to break down the black pawns' defense of the king (**A**).

22. Qg3+ Ng4

If the black king moves out of check, the white knight would check on g6, allowing a discovered attack on the black queen from the white queen (**B**).

(**A**)

(**B**)

23. Qxg4+ Kf8
The end is near (**C**).

24. Qf4 Resigns (**D**)
If Black plays f6 to stop mate on f7,
then Qxh6+ Ke8. Bg6++.

Black, a strong player, lost this game
without making any obvious
mistakes. White, having gradually
built up an attacking position, had to
crash through Black's defense with a
sacrifice. If this ploy had been
miscalculated, then Black may have
ended up the winner.

How to Improve

*"Chess is a sea in which a gnat may drink and
an elephant may bathe."*
Ancient Indian Proverb

TODAY CHESS is a young person's game. Traditionally it used to be considered an old man's game, something to relax over and enjoy in retirement, but that illusion has been completely shattered over the past few decades by gifted teenagers regularly becoming Grandmasters. It started in 1958 when a 15-year-old American, Bobby Fischer, became the youngest player ever to achieve this high standard of excellence. He went on to become world chess champion in 1972. The present Russian world champion, Garry Kasparov, also became a teenage Grandmaster in 1980 when he was only 17. Hungarian female child prodigy, Judit Polgar, obtained her Grandmaster title in 1991 when only 15 years and 5 months old, breaking Fischer's record. Judit is the youngest of three remarkable sisters who are all chess Grandmasters; the eldest, Zsuzsa, became women's world chess champion.

All these famous players had to start modestly. Bobby Fischer learned the moves from his elder sister. Garry Kasparov, whose father died when he was still a child, was encouraged and supported by his mother and his uncles. Judit Polgar had her chess-playing family to guide and support her natural chess talent.

Boris Spassky v. Bobby Fischer, 1972.

PRACTICE MAKES PERFECT

This is the vital first stage for improving your chess skills – find yourself a regular playing partner. Once the basic rules and moves of the pieces are understood, it is time to find others to play against, particularly some stronger players. Losing an occasional game should be the incentive to greater concentration. Finding more people with whom to play can often best be done either through friends and family, like the Polgars, or by joining a chess club, as Fischer and Kasparov did.

Chess clubs can be found in most towns. Many schools have their own chess clubs, as well as providing room for adult chess classes in the evenings. Some hotels, bars, and restaurants provide chess sets for their customers, while others are often the venues for chess club meetings. Many institutions, industries, and international companies have chess clubs and organize their own internal chess competitions. Joining a club will provide the right environment to encourage a continued improvement in chess skill and also make the game more socially stimulating. At this stage the chess books that it will suit you best to study should ideally be on the middle game, the endgame, and general opening theses.

The Competitive Streak

THE NEXT step in improving your chess is to start playing at a competitive level, no matter how elementary this may initially be. Chess tournaments started around the 1840s, being organized between regular players who would meet in fashionable chess coffee houses. In major cities like New York, London, Paris, and Berlin, coffee houses were popular venues for chess players to congregate. The players would organize individual matches to be played for a small stake, using seconds as if they were arranging a duel. One of the best-known coffee houses was the *Ries Divan* in London; by 1850 the players there, from many countries, were organizing tournaments between themselves.

In 1851 the first international tournament was held in London to coincide with the Great Exhibition. The best players came from Europe to match their skill against the English, particularly Howard Staunton who was the favorite. But the surprise winner was Adolf Anderssen, a

mathematics professor from Breslau, Germany. Anderssen went on to prove that he was one of the great players of his era.

In America, Europe, and Russia, chess tournaments are now very popular. Players have found them to be an excellent way to improve their game. In a weekend tournament, up to six rounds can be played. The results of each player are recorded for grading. This process is similar to recording scores to establish a golf handicap – it gives an indication of a player's playing strength. Every player in an officially organized tournament either has a rating, or is given a rating, and with each game played it alters: the rating goes up for a win, and down for a loss.

The World Chess Federation uses the Elo rating system. A good club player could expect a rating of 1700, an expert player 2000. Grandmasters are graded from 2500 upward, and a contender for the world championship, such as Nigel Short of England or India's Viswanathan Anand, have to be around 2700 to play against Garry Kasparov, the world champion since 1985.

CORRESPONDENCE CHESS
This is another valuable way to enjoy a game of chess and to learn through the experience. It is especially practical for those who, for various reasons, find it difficult to find a local opponent. It has the advantage of allowing you time to study the position on the board to try to find the best reply before you commit the move to paper and mail it to your distant adversary.

Chess computers have made competitive correspondence chess unsatisfactory, as there can be no verification as to whether the game is being played between the named players or their latest updated computers! But for friendly games it remains a fine way to play chess.

The latest way of playing correspondence chess is on the Internet, through e-mail. This is proving to be very popular as the cost of each move is modest, the game can be played at a much faster rate than by post, and the opponents are international.

Checkmates

YOU HAVE reached the end of the book. I hope that you have found it instructive and entertaining. Chess is a wonderful game, and it is my sincere wish that this introductory set will ignite your interest in it and lead you on to years of enjoyment. As a final test, practice by finding these checkmates on the next move.

And in these examples below, find the checkmates in two moves.

1. Qd8+ KxQ 2.Rf8++

Ne6++

1. Re7+ Kf8 2.RxR++

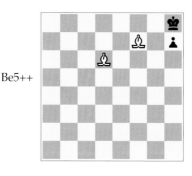

Be5++

Have fun!